A
Prayer

**Daily Prayer for Groups
and Individuals for
Morning, Evening
or any time of the day**

Liturgy
Office
ENGLAND
& WALES

CATHOLIC TRUTH SOCIETY
PUBLISHERS TO THE HOLY SEE

—— ❖ ——

A time of prayer is designed to be straightforward to use. It uses a simple format which can be followed everyday. It is for use by both individuals and groups. A form of Night Prayer is included for use at the end of the day on page 48.

Though some notes are given on pages 56-69 you may wish to start with the prayer itself either by getting familiar with the contents of the next few pages or by plunging in and beginning at the beginning. 'Lord, open our lips...'

—— ❖ ——

Acknowledgements

Psalms & Gospel Canticles © 1963 Grail. Texts from *The Divine Office* © Hierarchies of England and Wales, Ireland and Australia - AP Watt. Scripture Readings - NRSV. *Day is done* and *O God of light* by James Quinn SJ © Continuum. *Light of Gladness* © Paul Inwood. The rest © 2004 CBCEW. *Christian prayer is primarily...* Paul VI Apostolic Constitution promulgating the Divine Office, *Sacrificium Laudis* 8. *Those taking part...* GILH 19; *The purpose of the Office...* GILH 11. General Instruction on the Liturgy of the Hours (GILH).

Christian prayer is primarily the prayer of the entire human community joined to Christ. Each individual has their part in this prayer which is common to the one Body and it thus becomes the voice of the beloved Spouse of Christ, putting into words the wishes and desires of the whole Christian people and making intercession for the necessities common to all humankind.

Those taking part in the prayer should make it their own so that it becomes a source of devotion, abundant grace and nourishment for personal prayer and apostolic activity.

The purpose of the Office is to sanctify the day and all human activity.

Contents

A Time of Prayer

Structure

Introduction
  Opening Responses
  [Hymn]
Word
  [Seasonal Psalm]
  Psalm of the day
  Scripture Reading
  Reflection
  Gospel Canticle
Prayer
  Intercessions
  Lord's Prayer
  Concluding Prayer
  Blessing
  [ ] elements in brackets may be omitted
  Italic text - said by leader when used by a group.

Introduction

Structure

Opening Responses
[Hymn]

———————— ❖ ————————

At the beginning of a time of prayer we open ourselves to praise God in the name of the Trinity. We unite our prayer with the Church throughout the world.

———————— ❖ ————————

Opening Responses

Lord, open our lips.

And we shall praise your name.
Glory be to the Father, and to the Son,
and to the Holy Spirit.
As it was in the beginning, is now,
    and ever shall be,
world without end.
Amen.
Alleluia [Alleluia is omitted in Lent]

Hymns for Daily Prayer

Morning

O God of light, the dawning day
gives us new promise of your love.
Each fresh beginning is your gift,
like gentle dew from heaven above.

Your blessings, Father, never fail:
your Son, who is our daily bread,
the Holy Spirit of your love,
by whom each day your Church is led.

Make us the servants of your peace,
renew our strength, remove all fear;
be with us, Lord, throughout this day,
for all is joy if you are near.

To Father, Son and Spirit blest,
One only God, we humbly pray;
show us the splendour of your light
in death, the dawn of perfect day.

Text: James Quinn SJ
Tune: LM *for example* Tallis' Canon

Evening

Light of gladness, shining radiance
of the heavenly Father's face:
Jesus Christ, we greet you, bless you,
Holy Lord of saving grace.

As the day draws near its ending
sunlight dims with fading rays;
to the Father, Son and Spirit
now we sing our song of praise.

Son of God, the world's redeemer,
endless praises are your due;
Lord of life, may all creation
bring its joyful thanks to you.

Text: Paul Inwood
based on *Phos Hilaron* (2nd century)
Tune: 87 87 *for example* Love divine

Word

Structure

[Seasonal Psalm]
Psalm of the Day
Scripture Reading
Reflection
Gospel Canticle

❖

We pray with God's word through the psalms and a short reading. After a short period of silence we proclaim God's praise in the Gospel Canticle.

❖

Seasonal Psalm

Texts for the optional Seasonal Psalm can be
found on the following pages:

Psalm of the Day

A psalm and short scripture passage is
given for each day of the week.

SUNDAY

Psalm 150

Praise God in his holy place,
praise him in his mighty heavens.
Praise him for his powerful deeds,
praise his surpassing greatness.

O praise him with sound of trumpet,
praise him with lute and harp.
Praise him with timbrel and dance,
praise him with strings and pipes.

O praise him with resounding cymbals,
praise him with clashing of cymbals.
Let everything that lives and that breathes
give praise to the Lord.

Glory be to the Father, and to the Son,
and to the Holy Spirit,
as it was in the beginning, is now,
    and ever shall be,
world without end. Amen.

Scripture Reading

1 *Peter* 2:9-10

You are a chosen race, a royal priesthood, a holy nation, God's own people, in order that you may proclaim the mighty acts of him who called you out of darkness into his marvellous light. Once you were not a people, but now you are God's people; once you had not received mercy, but now you have received mercy.

Reflection

The reading is followed by a period of silent reflection

Gospel Canticle

MONDAY

Psalm 137 (138)

I thank you, Lord, with all my heart,
you have heard the words of my mouth.
In the presence of the angels I will bless you.
I will adore you before your holy temple.

I will thank you for you faithfulness and love
which excel all we ever knew of you.
On the day I called, you answered;
you increased the strength of my soul.

All earth's kings shall thank you
when they hear the words of your mouth.
They shall sing of the Lord's way:
'How great is the glory of the Lord!'

The Lord is high yet he looks on the lowly
and the haughty he knows from afar.
Though I walk in the midst of affliction
you give me life and frustrate my foes.

You stretch out your hand and save me,
your hand will do all things for me.
Your love, O Lord, is eternal,
discard not the work of your hands.

Glory be to the Father, and to the Son,
and to the Holy Spirit,
as it was in the beginning, is now,
   and ever shall be,
world without end. Amen.

Scripture Reading

Isaiah 55:10-11

For as the rain and the snow come down from heaven, and do not return there until they have watered the earth, making it bring forth and sprout, giving seed to the sower and bread to the eater, so shall my word be that goes out from my mouth; it shall not return to me empty, but it shall accomplish that which I purpose, and succeed in the thing for which I sent it.

Reflection

The reading is followed by a period of silent reflection

Gospel Canticle

TUESDAY

Psalm 42 (43)

> Defend me, O God, and plead my cause
> against a godless nation.
> From deceitful and cunning men
> rescue me, O God.
>
> Since you, O God, are my stronghold,
> why have you rejected me?
> Why do I go mourning
> oppressed by the foe?
>
> O send forth your light and your truth;
> let these be my guide.
> Let them bring me to you holy mountain
> to the place where you dwell.
>
> And I will come to the altar of God,
> the God of my joy.
> My redeemer, I will thank you on the harp,
> O God, my God.
>
> Why are you cast down my soul,
> why groan within me?
> Hope in God; I will praise him still,
> my saviour and my God.

Glory be to the Father, and to the Son,
and to the Holy Spirit,
as it was in the beginning, is now,
    and ever shall be,
world without end. Amen.

Scripture Reading

1 *Thessalonians* 5:16-18

Rejoice always, pray without ceasing, give thanks in all circumstances; for this is the will of God in Christ Jesus for you.

Reflection

The reading is followed by a period of silent reflection

Gospel Canticle

WEDNESDAY

Psalm 145

My soul, give praise to the Lord;
I will praise the Lord all my days,
make music to the God while I live.

Put no trust in princes,
in mortal men in whom there is no help.
Take their breath, they return to clay
and their plans that day come to nothing.

He is happy who is helped by Jacob's God,
whose hope is in the Lord his God,
who alone made heaven and earth,
the seas and all they contain.

It is he who keeps faith for ever,
who is just to those who are oppressed.
It is he who gives bread to the hungry,
the Lord, who sets prisoners free,

the Lord who gives sight to the blind,
who raises up those who are bowed down,
the Lord, who protects the stranger
and upholds the widow and orphan.

It is the Lord who loves the just
but thwarts the path of the wicked.
The Lord will reign for ever,
Sion's God, from age to age.

Glory be to the Father, and to the Son,
and to the Holy Spirit,
as it was in the beginning, is now,
    and ever shall be,
world without end. Amen.

Scripture Reading

Jeremiah 31:32

This is the covenant that I will make with the house
of Israel after those days, says the Lord: I will put my
law within them, and I will write it on their hearts;
and I will be their God, and they shall be my people.

Reflection

The reading is followed by a period of silent reflection

Gospel Canticle

THURSDAY

Psalm 22 (23)

The Lord is my shepherd;
there is nothing I shall want.
Fresh and green are the pastures
where he gives me respose.
Near restful waters he leads me,
to revive my drooping spirit.

He guides me along the right path;
he is true to his name.
If I should walk in the valley of darkness
no evil would I fear.
You are there with you crook and your staff;
with these you give me comfort.

You have prepared a banquet for me
in the sight of my foes.
My head you have anointed with oil;
my cup is overflowing.

Surely goodness and kindness
    shall follow me
all the days of my life.
In the Lord's own house shall I dwell
for ever and ever.

Glory be to the Father, and to the Son,
and to the Holy Spirit,
as it was in the beginning, is now,
    and ever shall be,
world without end. Amen.

Scripture Reading

Deuteronomy 10:12-13

What does the Lord your God require of you?
Only to fear the Lord your God, to walk in all his
ways, to love him, to serve the Lord your God
with all your heart and with all your soul.

Reflection

The reading is followed by a period of silent reflection

Gospel Canticle

FRIDAY

Psalm 14 (15)

Lord, who shall be admitted to your tent
and dwell on your holy mountain?

He who walks without fault;
he who acts with justice
and speaks the truth from his heart;
he who does not slander with his tongue;

he who does no wrong to his brother,
who casts no slur on his neighbour,
who holds the godless in disdain,
but honours those who fear the Lord;

he who keeps his pledge, come what may;
who takes no interest on a loan
and accepts no bribes against the innocent.
Such a man will stand firm for ever.

Glory be to the Father, and to the Son,
and to the Holy Spirit,
as it was in the beginning, is now,
    and ever shall be,
world without end. Amen.

Scripture Reading

Galatians 2:19-20

I have been crucified with Christ; and it is no longer I who live, but it is Christ who lives in me. And the life I now live in the flesh I live by faith in the Son of God, who loved me and gave himself for me.

Reflection

The reading is followed by a period of silent reflection

Gospel Canticle

SATURDAY

Psalm 8

How great is your name, O Lord our God,
through all the earth!

Your majesty is praised above the heavens;
on the lips of children and of babes
you have found praise to foil your enemy,
to silence the foe and the rebel.

When I see the heavens the world of your hands,
the moon and the stars which you arranged,
what is man that should keep him in mind,
mortal man that you care for him?

Yet you have made him little less than a god;
with glory and honour you crowned him,
gave him power over the works of your hand,
put all things under his feet.

All of them, sheep and cattle,
yes, even the savage beasts,
birds of the air, and fish
that make their way through the waters.

How great is your name, O Lord our God,
through all the earth!

Glory be to the Father, and to the Son,
and to the Holy Spirit,
as it was in the beginning, is now,
    and ever shall be,
world without end. Amen.

Scripture Reading

Romans 12:9-12

Let love be genuine; hate what is evil, hold fast to
what is good; love one another with mutual affection;
outdo one another in showing honour. Do not lag in
zeal, be ardent in spirit, serve the Lord. Rejoice in
hope, be patient in suffering, persevere in prayer.

Reflection

The reading is followed by a period of silent reflection

Gospel Canticle

Gospel Canticle for Morning

Canticle of Zechariah - *Benedictus*

Luke 1:68-79

Blessed be the Lord, the God of Israel!
He has visited his people and redeemed them.
He has raised up for us a mighty saviour
in the house of David his servant,

as he promised by the lips of holy men,
those who were his prophets from of old.
A saviour who would free us from our foes,
from the hands of all who hate us.

So his love for our fathers is fulfilled
and his holy covenant remembered.

He swore to Abraham our father to grant us
that, free from fear and saved from the hands
    of our foes,
we might serve him in holiness and justice
all the days of our life in his presence.
As for you, little child,
you shall be called a prophet of God,
    the Most High.

You shall go ahead of the Lord
to prepare his ways before him,

to make known to his people their salvation
through forgiveness of all their sins,
the loving kindness of the heart of our God
who visits us like the dawn from on high.

He will give light to those in darkness,
those who dwell in the shadow of death,
and guide us into the way of peace.

Glory be to the Father, and to the Son,
and to the Holy Spirit,
as it was in the beginning, is now,
    and ever shall be,
world without end. Amen.

In the afternoon the *Magnificat* may be used or
the Canticle may be omitted

Gospel Canticle for Evening

Canticle of Mary - *Magnificat*

Luke 1:46-55

My soul glorifies the Lord,
my spirit rejoices in God, my Saviour.
He looks on his servant in her lowliness;
henceforth all ages will call me blessed.

The Almighty works marvels for me.
Holy his name!
His mercy is from age to age,
on those who fear him.

He puts forth his arm in strength
and scatters the proud-hearted.
He casts the mighty from their thrones
and raises the lowly.

He fills the starving with good things,
sends the rich away empty.

He protects Israel, his servant,
remembering his mercy,
the mercy promised to our fathers,
to Abraham and his sons for ever.

Glory be to the Father, and to the Son,
and to the Holy Spirit,
as it was in the beginning, is now,
     and ever shall be,
world without end. Amen.

Prayer

Structure

Intercessions
Lord's Prayer
Concluding Prayer
Blessing

After reflecting on God's word and giving praise, we offer prayer for the world joining ourselves with the prayer of Christ in the Church.

Intercessions

Remember in your prayers
- The Church
- The world
- The local community
- Those in need
- In the evening it is traditional for the last intercession to be for the dead.

In the groups the following response may be used:
Lord, in your mercy:
Hear our prayer

Lord's Prayer

The Lord's Prayer can be introduced in these or similar words:

Let us pray to the Father, in the words our Saviour gave us:

Let us, once more, praise the Father and pray to him in the words of Christ himself, saying:

Our Father, who art in heaven,
hallowed be thy name.
Thy Kingdom come.
Thy will be done on earth, as it is in heaven.
Give us this day our daily bread,
and forgive us our trespasses,
as we forgive those who trespass against us
and lead us not into temptation,
but deliver us from evil.

Concluding Prayer

One of the following three prayers is said.

Let us praise you, Lord,
with voice and mind and deed;
and since life itself is your gift,
may all we have and are be yours.

We make our prayer
through our Lord Jesus Christ, your Son,
who lives and reigns with you
and the Holy Spirit,
one God, for ever and ever.
Amen.

———— ❖ ————

King of heaven and earth, Lord God,
rule over our hearts and bodies this day.
Sanctify us,
and guide our every thought, word and deed
according to the commandments of your law,
so that now and for ever
your grace may free and save us.

We make our prayer
through our Lord Jesus Christ, your Son,
who lives and reigns with you
and the Holy Spirit,
one God, for ever and ever.
Amen.

Lord, be the beginning and end
of all that we do and say.
Prompt our actions with your grace,
and complete them with your
 all-powerful help.

We make our prayer
through our Lord Jesus Christ, your Son,
who lives and reigns with you
and the Holy Spirit,
one God, for ever and ever.
Amen.

Blessing
*The Lord bless us and keep us from all evil,
and bring us to everlasting life.*
Amen.

Seasonal Psalm

ADVENT

Psalm 84 (85)

O Lord, you once favoured your land
and revived the fortunes of Jacob,
you forgave the guilt of your people
and covered all their sins.
You averted all your rage,
you calmed the heat of your anger.

Revive us now, God, our helper!
Put an end to your grievance against us.
Will you be angry with us for ever,
will your anger never cease?

Will you not restore again our life
that your people may rejoice in you?
Let us see, O Lord, your mercy
and give us your saving help.

I will hear what the Lord God has to say,
a voice that speaks of peace,
peace for his people and his friends
and those who turn to him in their hearts.
His help is near for those who fear him
and his glory will dwell in our land.

Mercy and faithfulness have met;
justice and peace have embraced.
Faithfulness shall spring from the earth
and justice look down from heaven.

The Lord will make us prosper
and our earth will yield its fruit.
Justice shall march before him
and peace shall follow his steps.

Glory be to the Father, and to the Son,
and to the Holy Spirit,
as it was in the beginning, is now,
    and ever shall be,
world without end. Amen.

Psalm of the Day page 12

CHRISTMAS

Psalm 97 (98)

> Sing a new song to the Lord
> for he has worked wonders.
> His right hand and his holy arm
> have brought salvation.
>
> The Lord has made known his salvation;
> has shown his justice to the nations.
> He remembered his truth and love
> for the house of Israel.
>
> All the ends of the earth have seen
> the salvation of our God.
> Shout to the Lord all the earth,
> ring out your joy.

Sing psalms to the Lord with the harp
with the sound of music.
With trumpets and the sound of the horn
acclaim the King, the Lord.

Let the sea and all within it, thunder;
the world, and all its peoples.
Let the rivers clap their hands
and the hills ring out their joy.
Rejoice at the presence of the Lord,
for he comes to rule the world with justice
and the peoples with fairness.

Glory be to the Father, and to the Son,
and to the Holy Spirit,
as it was in the beginning, is now,
    and ever shall be,
world without end. Amen.

Psalm of the Day page 12

LENT

Psalm 85 (86):1-13

Turn your ear, O Lord, and give answer
for I am poor and needy.
Preserve my life, for I am faithful:
save the servant who trusts in you.

You are my God, have mercy on me, Lord,
for I cry to you all the day long.
Give joy to your servant, O Lord,
for to you I lift up my soul.

O Lord, you are good and forgiving,
full of love to all who call.
Give heed, O Lord, to my prayer
and attend to the sound of my voice.

In the day of distress I will call
and surely you will reply.
Among the gods there is none like you,
    O Lord;
nor work to compare with yours.

All nations shall come to adore you
and glorify your name, O Lord:
for you are great and do marvellous deeds,
you who alone are God.
Show me, Lord, your way
so that I may walk in your truth.
Guide my heart to fear your name.

I will praise you, Lord my God,
    with all my heart
and glorify your name for ever;
for your love to me has been great:
you have saved me from the depths
    of the grave.

Glory be to the Father, and to the Son,
and to the Holy Spirit,
as it was in the beginning, is now,
    and ever shall be,
world without end. Amen.

Psalm of the Day page 12

EASTER

Psalm 117 (118):1-4, 15b-18, 22-29

Give thanks to the Lord for he is good,
for his love endures for ever.

Let the sons of Israel say:
'His love endures for ever.'
Let the sons of Aaron say:
'His love endures for ever.'
Let those who fear the Lord say:
'His love endures for ever.'

The Lord's right hand has triumphed;
his right hand raised me.
The Lord's right hand has triumphed;
I shall not die, I shall live
and recount his deeds.
I was punished, I was punished by the Lord,
but not doomed to die.

The stone which the builders rejected
has become the corner-stone.
This is the work of the Lord,
a marvel in our eyes.
This day was made by the Lord;
we rejoice and are glad.

O Lord, grant us salvation;
O Lord, grant success.
Blessed in the name of the Lord
is he who comes.
We bless you from the house of the Lord;
the Lord God is our light.

Go forward in procession with branches
even to the altar.
You are my God, I thank you.
My God, I praise you.
Give thanks to the Lord for he is good;
for his love endures for ever.

Glory be to the Father, and to the Son,
and to the Holy Spirit,
as it was in the beginning, is now,
    and ever shall be,
world without end. Amen.

Psalm of the Day page 12

SOLEMNITIES

Psalm 148:1-12

Praise the Lord from the heavens,
praise him in the heights.
Praise him, all his angels,
praise him, all his hosts.

Praise him, sun and moon,
praise him, shining stars.
Praise him, highest heavens
and the waters above the heavens.

Let them praise the name of the Lord.
He commanded: they were made.
He fixed them for ever,
gave a law which shall not pass away.

Praise the Lord from the earth,
sea creatures and all the oceans,
fire and hail, snow and mist,
stormy winds that obey his word;

all mountains and hills,
all fruit trees and cedars,
beasts, wild and tame,
reptiles and birds on the wing;

all earth's kings and peoples,
earth's princes and rulers;
young men and maidens,
old men together with children.

Glory be to the Father, and to the Son,
and to the Holy Spirit,
as it was in the beginning, is now,
    and ever shall be,
world without end. Amen.

Psalm of the Day page 12

FOR THE DEAD

Psalm 129 (130)

> Out of the depths I cry to you, O Lord,
> Lord, hear my voice!
> O let your ear be attentive
> to the voice of my pleading.
>
> If you, O Lord, should mark our guilt
> Lord, who would survive?
> But with you is found forgiveness;
> for this we revere you.
>
> My soul is waiting for the Lord,
> I count on his word.
> My soul is longing for the Lord
> more than watchman for daybreak.
> Let the watchman count on daybreak
> and Israel in the Lord.

Because with the Lord there is mercy
and fullness of redemption,
Israel indeed he will redeem
from all its iniquity.

Glory be to the Father, and to the Son,
and to the Holy Spirit,
as it was in the beginning, is now,
    and ever shall be,
world without end. Amen.

Psalm of the Day page 12

A Form of Night Prayer

Structure

Introduction
  Opening Responses
  Reflection
  [Hymn]

Word
  Psalm
  Scripture Reading
  Reflection
  [Response]
  Gospel Canticle

Prayer
  Concluding Prayer
  Blessing

  [ ] elements in brackets may be omitted.

Introduction

Opening Responses

O God, come to our aid.

O Lord, make haste to help us.
Glory be to the Father, and to the Son,
and to the Holy Spirit,
as it was in the beginning, is now,
   and ever shall be,
world without end. Amen.
Alleluia [Alleluia is omitted in Lent]

Reflection

A time of silent reflection looking at the day that has gone:
to give thanks and to seek forgiveness.

Hymn

If a hymn is not sung it is omitted.

1. Day is done, but Love unfailing
   dwells ever here;
   shadows fall, but hope, prevailing,
   calms every fear.
   Loving Father, none forsaking,
   take our hearts, of Love's own making,
   watch our sleeping, guard our waking,
   be always near!

2. Dark descends, but Light unending
   shines through our night;
   you are with us, ever lending
   new strength to sight;
   one in love, your truth confessing,
   one in hope of heaven's blessing,
   may we see, in love's possessing,
   love's endless light!

3. Eyes will close, but you, unsleeping,
   watch by our side;
   death may come: in love's safe keeping
   still we abide.
   God of love, all evil quelling,
   sin forgiving, fear dispelling,
   stay with us, our hearts indwelling,
   this eventide!

James Quinn, SJ
Tune: 84 84 88 84 *for example* Ard hyd y nos

Word

Psalm

Psalm 133 (134)

O come, bless the Lord,
all you who serve the Lord,
who stand in the courts of the Lord,
in the courts of the house of our God.

Lift up your hands to the holy place
and bless the Lord through the night.
May the Lord bless you from Sion,
he who made both heaven and earth.

Glory be to the Father, and to the Son,
and to the Holy Spirit,
as it was in the beginning, is now,
    and ever shall be,
world without end. Amen.

Scripture Reading

Deuteronomy 6: 4-7

Hear, O Israel: The Lord is our God, the Lord
alone. You shall love the Lord your God with all
your heart, and with all your soul, and with all
your might. Keep these words that I am
commanding you today in your heart. Recite
them to your children and talk about them
when you are at home and when you are away,
when you lie down and when you rise.

Reflection

The reading is followed by a pause for reflection.

Response

[The following response may be used with groups.

Into your hands, Lord, I commend my spirit.
Into your hands, Lord, I commend my spirit.

You have redeemed us, Lord God of truth.
Into your hands, Lord, I commend my spirit.

Glory be to the Father, and to the Son,
and to the Holy Spirit.
Into your hands, Lord, I commend my spirit.]

Gospel Canticle

[The following antiphon may be used before
and after the canticle.
Save us, Lord, while we are awake;
protect us while we sleep;
that we may keep watch with Christ
and rest with him in peace.]

At last, all-powerful Master,
you give leave to your servant
to go in peace, according to your promise.

For my eyes have seen your salvation
which you have prepared for all nations,
the light to enlighten the Gentiles
and give glory to Israel, your people.

Glory be to the Father, and to the Son,
and to the Holy Spirit,
as it was in the beginning, is now,
    and ever shall be,
world without end. Amen.

Prayer

Concluding Prayer
Visit this house, we pray you, Lord:
drive far away from it all the snares
of the enemy.
May your holy angels stay here and guard
us in peace,
and let your blessings be always upon us.
Through Christ our Lord.
Amen.

Blessing
The Lord grant us a quiet night
and a perfect end.
Amen.

Notes

Notes

Introduction

This resource provides a simple, traditional structure which can be used by groups or individuals at any time during the day. Either praying alone or as a small group it unites us in prayer with the Church throughout the world.

In the prayer praise and thanksgiving is given to God for all that he has done for us. Prayer is offered too for the needs of the ourselves and the world.

The structure of the prayer follows the pattern of the Liturgy of the Hours. It has been simplified so that through the repetition of familiar texts these texts can become embedded in people's lives and prayer. This practice reflects an early form of the Prayer of the Church where the community would come together at morning and evening to sing and pray psalms and other texts which did not vary from week to week.

A Celebration of Time

This resource is intended to be used at any time of the day. It is for those who are looking for a daily time of prayer and wish to be united with the wider Church. It can be used as a form of Morning or Evening Prayer. Some will make time on a journey to work or a lunch break.

There are options in the prayer to choose depending on the time of day. When it is prayed in the morning the Canticle of Zechariah, the *Benedictus* is used; in the evening the Canticle of Mary, the *Magnificat*. The broader sweep of the time - the liturgical year is marked by the inclusion of a seasonal psalm.

Night Prayer, which is intended for use at the end of the day, is provided on page 48. With its opportunity for reflection on the day it has a different focus than prayer during the day.

A Time for Prayer - Structure

For clarity the liturgy has been given three sections: **Introduction**, **Word** and **Prayer**.

Introduction

Opening Responses

At the beginning of the prayer we are invited to join in the praise of God. It is customary to make the Sign of the Cross as we say the Opening Responses.

Hymn

A hymn can be chosen according to the Liturgical Season, the time of day or on a general theme of praise and thanksgiving. Hymns are intended to be sung; if the hymn is not sung it is best omitted. An example of a morning and an evening hymn can be found on pages 8-9.

Further examples can be found on the Liturgy Office website (*www.liturgyoffice.org.uk/Resources*)

Word

Psalmody

Psalms are at the heart of the Prayer of the Church. Psalms are poems in praise of God that express a wide variety of emotions. There are a variety of ways of reciting the psalms, a number of which are noted in the section Praying as a Group. Above all they should be prayed with open hearts.

During the the doxology (Glory be...) it is customary to bow the head.

Two psalms are provided: a psalm of the day and a seasonal psalm.

Seasonal Psalm

A psalm is provided for the liturgical seasons of Advent, Christmas, Lent and Easter. One is also provided for Solemnities - days of special celebration such as St Peter and St Paul, and one to commemorate the Dead.

This first psalm is optional and may be omitted.

Psalm of the Day

A psalm is provided for every day of the week. It is hoped that through repetition these texts will known by heart.

Scripture Reading

A short text is provided each day.
There are a number of other possibilities.

- To choose one of the readings from the Mass of the day, either the first reading or the Gospel.

- To take the opportunity to reflect on the Sunday readings: in preparation from Thursday to Saturday; in reflection from Monday to Wednesday.

- To follow a systematic reading of a book of the bible.

Reflection

The scripture reading is followed by a period of silent reflection. To reflect on the word that has been heard and to prepare for the intercessions.

Gospel Canticle

In the Morning the Canticle of Zechariah - the *Benedictus* is proclaimed; in the Evening the Canticle of Mary - the *Magnificat*.

In the afternoon the *Magnificat* may be used or the Canticle may be omitted.

Prayer

Intercessions

In the Liturgy of Hours our prayer is united with the whole Church through Christ. Suggestions are given of themes for prayer. Some may prefer to use other resources such as the Divine Office.

Lord's Prayer

The intercessions are concluded by the Lord's Prayer.

Concluding Prayer

A number of final collects are provided. This prayer can be replace with a prayer from another source such as the Divine Office.

Blessing

The time of prayer concludes with a blessing.

Praying by Yourself

A time of prayer has been prepared so that it can be used by individuals as well as groups who wish to join in the prayer of the Church and would appreciate a short, simple format.

First time use

Take time to become familiar with the structure of prayer and the choices that you can make. Though this booklet contains a complete set of texts for use you may decide you want to supplement it with other resources particularly with regard to the scripture reading: e.g. a lectionary or missal, or a bible.

Space

You may wish to prepare a space for your prayer, somewhere you can be comfortable and undisturbed. You may wish to use a visual focus such as an icon, image or candle.

Preparation

Before you begin to pray take a moment's stillness. Recall all the things you wish to praise and thank God for today.

Psalmody

You may wish to vary your ways of praying the psalms by taking time to reflect on a number of verses each day rather than the whole psalm.

Praying as a Group

A time for prayer can be used by a variety of groups. It could provide a form of Morning Prayer for parishes where Mass is not celebrated everyday but people wish to come together to pray. It provides a simple form of prayer for parish meetings or catechetical sessions. For groups reflecting on scripture together it could offer a structure for a session with the discussion following on from the silent reflection.

Preparation

Before praying together the prayer needs to be prepared. Choices about the choices of psalms and hymn; the scripture reading and the form of the intercessions need to be made. People need to be asked to be ministers.

Ministers

When praying together it is good if the different ministries are shared among the group. To celebrate together you will need:

- someone to lead - to open and close the prayer texts said by the leader alone are shown in *italic*;
- someone to read;
- a musician, if possible.

Space

Where you pray will depend on the circumstances of the group. It may be helpful to provide a focus for prayer: an icon, image or candle.

Posture

It is customary to stand for the Introduction, to sit for the psalms and the scripture reading, to stand for the Gospel Canticle until the end of the prayer.

Music

It is good to sing some of the prayer. A confident cantor can lead the singing of the psalms, the gospel canticle and the hymn.

Psalmody

The psalms can be sung or said in a number of ways. The most familiar way is for those praying to be divided into two groups and each group to recite an alternate verse back and forth. The psalm could be read by everyone all together or some groups may value it being read well by just one voice with all joining in the doxology.

Scripture Reading

Where the prayer is being used in place of Mass it would be appropriate to choose one of the readings from the Mass of the day, either the first reading or the Gospel.

Reflection

As noted above after a time of silence the group may wish to share a reflection on the reading.

Intercessions

People can be invited to pray for their need and the needs of the world. It is important that the group's prayer reflects the needs of the wider community.

Blessing

Some groups may wish to end with a sign of peace.

A Form of Night Prayer

This simple form of Night Prayer can be used by individuals and groups. It is intended for single occasions rather than daily use. For more regular use Night Prayer from the Divine Office is recommended.

Structure

For clarity the liturgy has been given three sections: **Introduction**, **Word** and **Prayer**.

Introduction

Opening Responses

At the beginning of the prayer we are invited to join in the praise of God.

Reflection

Night Prayer begins with a reflection on the day.

Hymn

Another hymn may be used in place of the one given. It can be chosen according to the Liturgical Season, the time of day or on a general theme of praise and thanksgiving. Hymns are intended to be sung; if it is not sung it is best omitted.

Word

Psalmody

Psalms are at the heart of the Prayer of the Church. Psalms are poems in praise of God that express a wide variety of emotions. There are a variety of ways of reciting the psalms, a number of which are noted in the section Praying as a Group (pg. 64), above all they should be prayed with open hearts.

Scripture Reading

A short text is provided. There are a number of other possibilities are suggested on page 61.

Reflection

The scripture reading is followed by a period of silent reflection.

A short response is provided which can be used when praying as a group.

Gospel Canticle

At Night Prayer the Canticle of Simeon is proclaimed. The antiphon may be used when praying as a group.

Prayer

Concluding Prayer

A final collect is provided.

Blessing

Night Prayer concludes with a blessing.

Praying by Yourself

See the notes on page 63.

Praying as a Group

The notes on page 64 will be useful.